GUARDSMAN ON HORSEBACK WITH RAISED SWORD

THE FORBES COLLECTION

TOY SOLDIERS

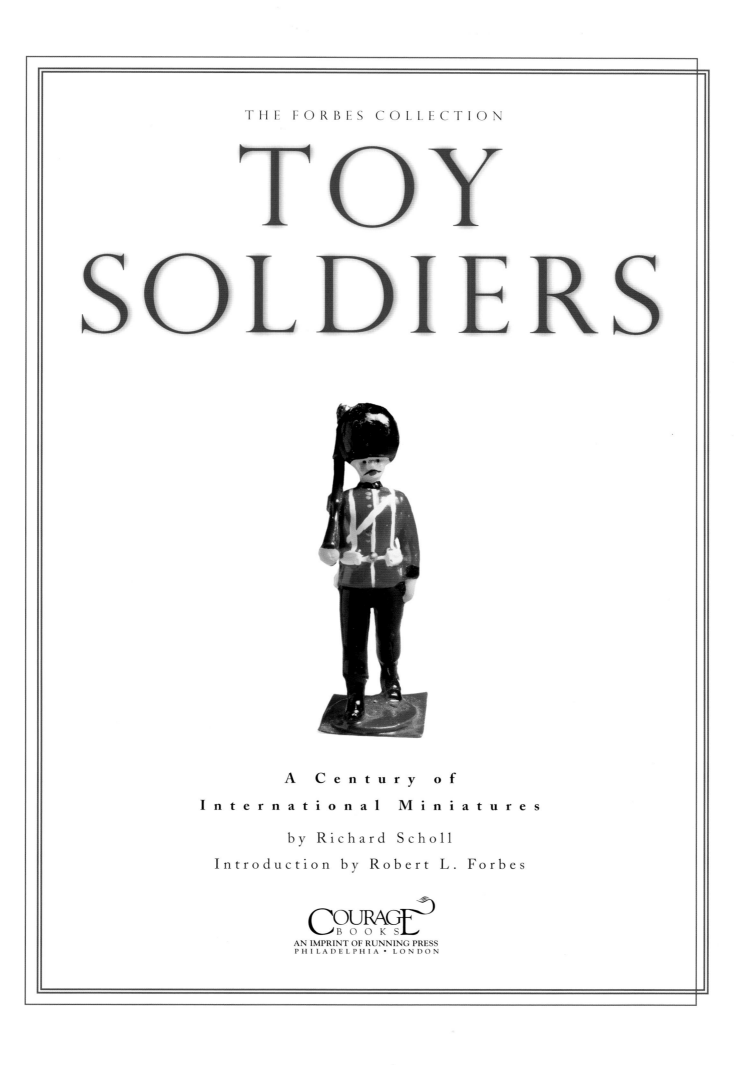

A Century of

International Miniatures

by Richard Scholl

Introduction by Robert L. Forbes

COURAGE BOOKS

AN IMPRINT OF RUNNING PRESS
PHILADELPHIA • LONDON

©2004 Forbes Inc.

The Forbes Collection™ is a trademark owned by Forbes
Management Co. Inc. Its use is pursuant to a license agreement.
All rights reserved.

All rights reserved under the Pan-American and International
Copyright Conventions

Printed in China

This book may not be reproduced in whole or in part, in any form or
by any means, electronic or mechanical, including photocopying,
recording, or by any information storage and retrieval system now
known or hereafter invented, without written permission from the
publisher.

9   8   7   6   5   4   3   2   1

Digit on the right indicates the number of this printing

Library of Congress Control Number: 2004105753

ISBN 0-7624-1879-6

Cover design by Frances Soo Ping Chow and Gwen Galeone
Interior design by Frances Soo Ping Chow and Gwen Galeone
Edited by Jennifer Leczkowski
Typography: Abadi, ACaslon and Perpetua

This book may be ordered by mail from the publisher.
But try your bookstore first!

Published by Courage Books, an imprint of
Running Press Book Publishers
125 South Twenty-second Street
Philadelphia, Pennsylvania 19103-4399

Visit us on the web!
www.runningpress.com

TABLE OF CONTENTS

(Above) World War II Soldiers

ACKNOWLEDGMENTS

This book simply could not have been completed without the hospitality and aid of the staff at the Forbes Galleries in New York. The author wishes to thank Margaret Kelly Trombly, Vice President of the Forbes Collection, and her staff, who made their voluminous files available for the research needed to complete this book. The author is also indebted to Gabrielle Schickler, Curator; Bonnie S. Kirschstein, Managing Director; and Allison Beth Sawczyn, Office Coordinator. The agent representing The Forbes Collection™, Joan G. Stanley of J.G. Stanley & Co., Inc., was invaluable as a liaison between the Forbes Galleries and both the publisher and the author. The author also wishes to express heartfelt gratitude to a couple who were instrumental in building the Forbes collection of toy soldiers and became co-curators of the first museum to house the collection: Anne Johnson and her late husband, Peter, who wrote *Toy Armies*, one of the most important books ever written about toy soldiers, which includes considerable information and insight into the Forbes Collection. The author drew heavily on this book as well as many other writings by Peter Johnson, who was one of the most knowledgeable and well respected experts on toy soldier collecting. We also wish to thank Larry Stein and Paul Rider for their vivid photography of the toy soldier displays housed in the Forbes Galleries. The publisher, Running Press, was represented by Jennifer Leczkowski, who provided essential editorship and coordination of the photos. The author also wishes to thank Robert Forbes for his superb introduction and insightful answers to questions posed in an interview that is presented in its entirety within these pages.

Note: The Forbes Galleries are located at 62 Fifth Avenue, New York City, and are open free to the public Tuesday through Saturdays, 10 A.M. to 4 P.M. Thursdays are for groups by appointment only.

In describing the evolution of the collection, some soldiers may be mentioned that have been sold or decommissioned. However, rest assured that all the soldiers shown in the photographs in this book are on display at the Forbes Galleries in New York City.

Spanish Heyde-like solids from 1914 representing the regiment Fernando in gala uniforms.

THE TOY SOLDIER GALLERY

Several thousand miniature troops from The Forbes Collection are assembled in the toy soldier gallery. The history of the toy soldier is presented in a series of dioramas and vignettes featuring the work of Britains, Heyde, Mignot, Elastolin, and other manufacturers.

THE LAND
OF COUNTERPANE

· · ·

BY ROBERT LOUIS STEVENSON (1850–94)

When I was sick and lay a-bed,
    I had two pillows at my head,
And all my toys beside me lay
    To keep me happy all the day.

And sometimes for an hour or so
    I watched my leaden soldiers go,
With different uniforms and drills,
    Among the bed-clothes, through the hills;

And sometimes sent my ships in fleets
    All up and down among the sheets;
Or brought my trees and houses out,
    And planted cities all about.

I was the giant great and still
    That sits upon the pillow-hill,
And sees before him, dale and plain,
    The pleasant land of counterpane.

Land of Counterpane Jessie Wilcox Smith oil and charcoal on board **22" x 14"**

INTRODUCTION

by Robert L. Forbes

My father was an avid collector of many things in his lifetime, but, curiously, these collections were never started with the idea of amassing a significant amount of whatever it was, from Fabergé eggs to toy soldiers. He would buy something he liked, that tickled his fancy or, in this case, that reminded him of the toy armies he had as a young boy. When he bought his first batch later in life, he was at an auction to buy something else (he loved auctions for their lively market atmosphere). Up came a lot—a box of soldiers, somewhat beat up and yet to him appealing. So as he put it, "Up went my hand and it has stayed mostly up ever since."

I remember him telling me about the purchase and it reminded me of when my brothers and I were but wee lads ourselves and were the delighted recipients of our own armies camped under the Christmas tree. Like my Dad's, our armies saw many a campaign, and like his, slowly vanished into that nether world where childhood playthings seem to go, so when he proudly showed me his newest acquisitions, I could easily relate to his excitement.

That sparkle in his eye, though, told me it was unlikely that this would be the last of his lead-cast recruits. And sure enough, the army grew and grew.

I was with him once in London, making the rounds of antique stores, and we visited the myriad small antique stalls in a grand hall called Antiquarius. We stopped and chatted with a very pleasant and toy-soldier-knowledgeable couple named Peter and Anne Johnson. Dad noted their names and bought a few pieces. Little did any of us expect then that the Johnsons were to play a large part in our collecting life.

On subsequent trips, he would stop there, and soon what

A HORSE-RACING SCENE

THE PROUD PAGEANTRY OF FORBES' TOY LEGIONS

Perhaps it is the thrill of command of their courageous ever vigilant attitude, but whatever the reason, toy soldiers have long captured the imaginations of children and adults alike. Through the ages small-scale warriors of varied construction have valiantly responded to the orders of civilian generals, be they delivered in ancient Greek or medieval German or modern English. Stalwart legions still bravely battle enemies, real and imagined, in nurseries, backyards, beach heads—every known terrain. Their ranks often thinned by casualties, their shiny coats reflecting the ravages of time, the gallant soldiers fight on undaunted.

SAWDUST ARMIES

Over the years toy soldiers have been made in a variety of materials: tin, lead, aluminum alloys, paper, and plastic. Warriors made of a composition of sawdust and glue were as familiar to generations of American youths as they were to those of Germany through two world wars. This display in the Forbes Galleries of both new and old toy soldiers shows how the history of the toy soldier is still being written.

was an itch to be occasionally scratched became a major case of collector-itis. True to form, Dad did what was his wont—pay what was necessary to get the best and never look back. When he died in 1990, his army stood at more than 70,000 strong, not only reflecting hundreds of examples from most of the great manufacturers, but also including many dioramas featuring models made by hand and crafted to fit into a specific scene.

Dad loved nothing more than having a project, where the anticipation was as much fun as the pursuit and attainment of the goal. The quest for toy soldiers gave him this in spades when he realized what a daunting task it would be to assemble a definitive collection, containing one of every type of set made. So he learned to be selective and to go for the pieces that struck his fancy.

While the collection has a number of civilian scenes, Dad's main interest was in the soldiers, even though he was not one who celebrated war. It was history he pursued alongside his reclamation of childhood. As a young man, he fought in World War II. He landed in France about six weeks after D-Day and made his way as a staff sergeant in charge of a machine gun unit all the way to Germany, where he was badly wounded just before the Battle of the Bulge. He recovered for ten months in a hospital and for the rest of his life carried a slight limp from the machine-pistol bullet that passed through his leg. He was proud of the Purple Heart and Bronze Star he was awarded for his actions. Yet he was never afraid that toy soldiers or toy guns would cause vio-

WHILE THE COLLECTION HAS A NUMBER OF CIVILIAN SCENES, DAD'S MAIN INTEREST WAS IN THE SOLDIERS, EVEN THOUGH HE WAS NOT ONE WHO CELEBRATED WAR

SAWDUST ARMIES (DETAIL)

lence in children; for him, war was a fact of life. He always encouraged us to make up our own minds about any issue. He just never felt exposure to such playthings would naturally lead to gunpowder as the solution to settle arguments. In fact, he encouraged us to do just the opposite—use our heads and our education to solve confrontations.

Gathering his troops was fun for Dad, and figuring out how to display them was the next logical step. Finding the right place to display his soldiers quickly followed hiring the Johnsons. Having bought a palace in Tangier, Morocco, for the headquarters of an Arabic edition of *Forbes* magazine years earlier, he realized this would be a great place for the soldiers, with lots of room to grow into. So off the toy soldiers went to become the largest standing army in North Africa. Then Dad was approached by the National Geographic Society to lend them some soldiers for display in their galleries in Washington, D.C. With the expert design of Peter Purpura and Gary Kisner, about 10,000 pieces were arranged into various scenes.

Accompanied by historical notes by the Johnsons, the show was a huge success—so much so that my father didn't want it to end. The scenes from that exhibition are what you now see in this book. Dad simply said he wanted the first floor of the Forbes building in New York City to be a public gallery that could house the fabulous displays mounted at the National Geographic Society building. And not just the soldiers, but also the toy boat display Purpura and Kisner had created earlier. So those 10,000 soldiers and their civilian compatriots found a permanent billet at 62 Fifth Avenue in New York. Joining them were not just the toy boats but the Monopoly® games, as well as display space for rotating shows of the magazine's presidential and United States manuscript collection.

Two weeks of dinners and press events heralded the opening of the galleries, and Dad never tired of taking the many moguls who lunched at Forbes through the galleries,

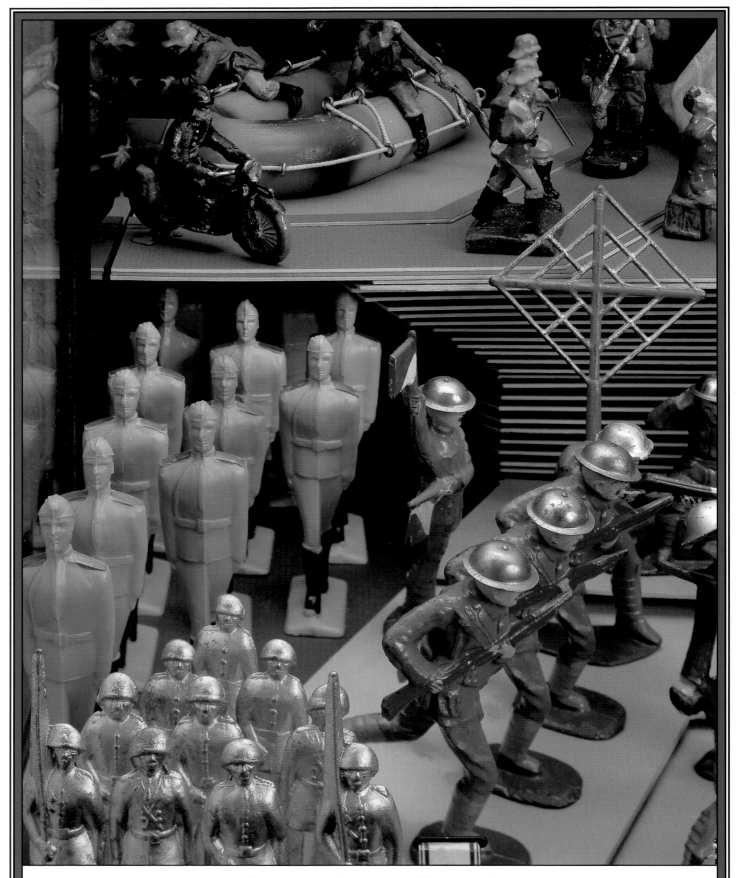

SAWDUST ARMIES (DETAIL)

Purchased by Malcolm Forbes during a motorcycle trip across the USSR in the summer of 1979; Forbes was amazed to find these modern Soviet soldiers made from metal and plastic.

DOUGHBOYS

These dime-store doughboys are typical of the crude but charming soldiers manufactured
by Barclay and Manoil in the United States during the 1930s and 1940s.

sharing his delightful personal thoughts on the pieces shown.

On a personal note, I recall that on a motorcycle trip to Russia we made in 1979, I bought some Russian toy soldiers to bring home for my son to play with. There were two types, green plastic ones and stiff-standing lead-cast models painted gold. When Dad saw them he asked—pleaded—they be made part of the displays then being constructed. I was delighted to share them with the world, but I brought my son a few other goodies from the Soviet Union to make up for this, rest assured!

While my real interest lay with the toy boat collection, I still took pleasure in what my father had done with the soldiers. After his death, my brothers and I eventually decided to sell off the soldiers in Morocco, glad to return them to the public via the auction rooms where so many had come from. It felt right to give a new generation of collectors the chance to "play" with them after the Forbes family had enjoyed them for so long.

But the remaining soldiers and marching bands, cowboys and Indians, Aztecs and sailors, farmers and fox hunters, and kings and queens now on display at the Forbes Galleries are on parade for you in the following pages. They are offered as a vision of a child's world supplanted by a faster-paced race of action toys and electronic gadgets, videos and television. So walk with us through this book, while letting your imagination play again. Or, even better, sit down with a youngster and share this experience together. It worked well for me and for my father before me.

GERMAN FLATS

These handsomely painted flats are from a set of Huns battling Gauls, produced in the twentieth century by the German firm of Ochel.

CHAPTER 1:

WHO COLLECTS TOY SOLDIERS?

"WHEN I SEE THEM ALL ON PARADE, I GET A REMINISCENT JOY. I GET AS ENTHUSED AS I DID WHEN I SAW THEM IN TOY STORES AS A CHILD."

—Malcolm Forbes

On Parade

In the park a gazebo with military band by Under Two Flags, London is performing while a lady feeding birds, a policeman, boy with a sailing boat, dogs, and other men, women, and children enjoy the day. In the forefront, pipers of the Scottish Regiment by Britains and the Royal Army Service Corps band by Pestana march by.

British Indian Army Soldier

A 19th Bengal Lancer from the British Indian Army by Harold Pestana from Soldiers of the Queen.

BRITAINS PIPER

A piper of the Highland Regiment by Britains.

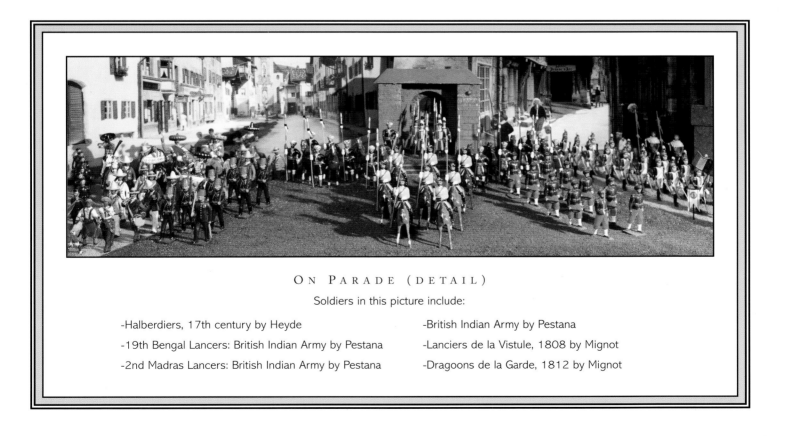

ON PARADE (DETAIL)

Soldiers in this picture include:

-Halberdiers, 17th century by Heyde

-19th Bengal Lancers: British Indian Army by Pestana

-2nd Madras Lancers: British Indian Army by Pestana

-British Indian Army by Pestana

-Lanciers de la Vistule, 1808 by Mignot

-Dragoons de la Garde, 1812 by Mignot

On Parade (detail)

Harold Pestana, a Maine geology professor, produced his own army entitled Soldiers of the Queen. They are modern models that represent Queen Victoria's Army in the late nineteenth century and are based on the figures of Britains, the leading British toy soldier manufacturer.

Here Pestana's Soldiers of the Queen are part of a wiring party at work. One soldier climbs a pole while the others feed him wire from a reel on the back of a horse-drawn wagon. For the label on each box of his soldiers, Pestana purloined an image of Victoria from a bottle of Bombay Gin.

These Soldiers of the Queen were produced in very limited numbers. Some are copies of old Britains, some are made from master figures that were modifications of old Britains, and some are original figures whose masters were made from scratch or by extensive conversion of metal and plastic figures. All units, with one or two exceptions, come in dark red cardboard boxes. The Soldiers of the Queen box label was designed by Professor W. B. Miller of the Colby College Art Department.

In ancient times, little warriors were made of wood. Crude toy soldiers were found in Egyptian tombs of the Eleventh Dynasty, which flourished more than 2,000 years before the birth of Christ. These little titans encompassed a full complement of militia—infantry, cavalry, charioteers, and archers. Historians also concur that little soldiers were crafted—and probably played with—by the children of ancient Roman, Greek, Etruscan, and Viking civilizations. And archaeologists have unearthed tiny replicas of the famed Trojan horse.

"Legend has it that, when a boy, the Holy Roman Empire's Maximilian I had a collection of tiny knights, impeccably engraved and cast in bronze, with which he staged play tournaments and jousts on a tabletop," art historian John Dornberg recollected in an article in *Museum* magazine in 1982.

To devise ingenious battle plans and dramatically revamp Dutch military strategy, William of Orange employed thousands of toy soldiers in various formations. It has been said that two kings of France—Louis XIII and Louis XIV—amassed large armies of toy soldiers when they were children.

Some were wrought of solid silver; others were fashioned of tin and pewter by German craftsmen. (Louis XIV later had his silver soldiers melted down to finance his real wars.)

"Russia's Czar Peter III, the luckless husband of Catherine the Great, had a collection so vast that he built an entire château just to house it. And Czar Nicholas I ordered replicas of all members of his horse guard regiment cast in miniature and meticulously hand-painted by Ernst Heinrichsen, a renowned nineteenth-century Nüremberg master of this art," reported Dornberg.

Some metal toy soldiers also have survived from medieval Europe. History shows that in 1516, Emperor Maximilian I commissioned an armorer from Austria to fashion a pair of miniature knights equipped with lances and mounted on wooden horses. The emperor wanted them as gifts for the child king of Hungary, Ludwig II.

In his autobiography, Johann Wolfgang von Goethe (1749–1832) wrote about how he played with toy soldiers in his youth. Other writers who loved their little soldiers included Charlotte and Emily Brontë, Robert Louis Stevenson, and H.G. Wells, whose book *Little Wars* describes toy

"TOY SOLDIERS HAVE PROBABLY BEEN AROUND AS LONG AS THE WORLD HAS HAD ARMIES."

Rita Reif, *The New York Times*

LANDING PARTY

A landing party of the Boer War support ship, H.M.S. *Terrible*, made by putting together a Britains navel gun, Royal Horse Artillery limber, and non-military cattle.

MEDICAL CORPS

The Royal Army Medical Corps by Britains. The colorful line was very popular for the firm.

GUNS AND ARTILLERY

Several fine examples of military guns and artillery made by various companies.

THE GENUINE GIANT OF TOY SOLDIER COLLECTING
WAS THE EBULLIENT, ENERGETIC, AND ALWAYS
ENTERTAINING MALCOLM FORBES

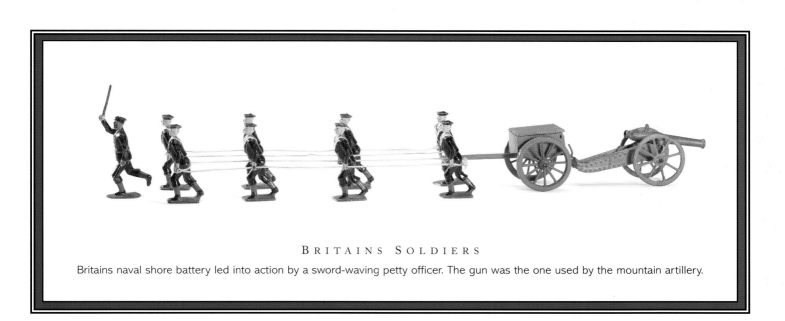

BRITAINS SOLDIERS

Britains naval shore battery led into action by a sword-waving petty officer. The gun was the one used by the mountain artillery.

war games. Toy soldiers play an important role in the E.T.A. Hoffmann classic fantasy novel *The Nutcracker and the Mouse King*. What's more, Hans Christian Andersen wrote two fairy tales about tin soldiers.

Winston Churchill collected toy soldiers, as did Douglas Fairbanks, Jr., and the American artist Andrew Wyeth. But the genuine giant of toy soldier collecting was the ebullient, energetic, and always entertaining Malcolm Forbes. And no one built a collection quite like Forbes.

"Mrs. Anne Johnson was a dealer in antique toys and she first met Forbes when she sold him a marching band," *The*

Washington Times reported on November 19, 1982. Peter Johnson was a part-time London copy editor and freelance writer whose "avocation was toy soldiering."

Malcolm Forbes used to visit the antique shop owned by Anne Johnson. Called the Lead Soldier, the shop was located in the Antiquarius, an antiques supermarket on King's Road in London. "For the most part, Malcolm's buys were random and disappointingly small but Anne Johnson, the shop owner, thought, quite forgivably, that one day he might go potty and buy the lot." (*Now!*, 1979.)

One day, instead of purchasing a soldier or two, Forbes

did acquire the entire lot. At the time, Anne didn't know his identity. To her, he was simply an American who asked for army marching bands. "Although I didn't have any," she said in an article in *The Standard* in 1981, ". . . I knew there were a few at my house. When I mentioned this he practically begged to be allowed to come and see them." Anne was reluctant to do business in her home, so she called her husband. Peter Johnson consented and Forbes came to the Johnsons' home and stayed for two hours, talking about toy soldiers and forgetting that he was racking up a cab fare.

Peter Johnson said the collection was remarkable for two reasons, in "The Forbes Collection," an article that appeared in *Military Modellings* in 1979: "First, the collection is eclectic, cutting across the boundaries of period, type, makers, nationality, and any other classification you care to name in the field of soldier collecting. Most keen collectors . . . limit themselves to a theme; it can be old toys or modern models,

full-round, semi or flat, Britains . . . Mignot, Heyde, representational of a given period, country or war, transport and support troops, or any of a host of options. The Forbes collection has the lot. It is heavily accented on the old toy lead soldier . . . but in its scope it is probably unique among major collections because of its near-comprehensive coverage of this area. Few collectors, having expended much time and money on amassing large collections, have either the space or the resources to put their soldiers on effective and extravagant display."

In an article in *The New York Times* on July 25, 1982, Rita Reif wrote: "Toy soldiers have probably been around as long as the world has had armies. And they have been collected passionately for centuries. Only over the last decade, however, has an assemblage of toy soldiers become important enough to fill a museum and become subject matter for a book."

WHAT ARE THEY MADE OF AND WHO MADE THEM?

Some people think they're made of tin; some think they're crafted of lead. They're both right and wrong. Tin is too brittle and lead is too soft, but a mixture produces a semi-flexible soldier ideal for capturing intricate details. For this reason, alloys were used by commercial toy soldier makers from the early nineteenth through the twentieth century.

Among the rarest antique soldiers are those made in European workshops during the Napoleonic wars. But the center of the toy soldier industry was the southern German city of Nüremberg. Founded in 1839, the firm of Heinrichsen was particularly instrumental in the growth of the toy soldier collecting phenomenon.

Various German and French companies led the way in producing toy soldiers until a British toy maker—appropriately named William Britain—introduced the revolutionary hollow-cast figure in 1893. Britain's molds were usually made of two pieces bolted together. With a quick, deft movement, excess metal was poured out of the mold before it could set. The result was a light, cheap soldier that could be sold at low prices. Soon the firm of Britains dominated the landscape of imaginative toy soldiers.

Thousands of Britains' soldiers—as well as those of many other manufacturers—are among the vast army that fascinates those who visit the Forbes Galleries in New York City. The galleries there occupy the entire first floor of the *Forbes* magazine building.

WHAT DO TOY SOLDIER COLLECTORS CARE ABOUT?

Steve Balkin ran the Burlington Antique Toy Shop from a balcony in a New York City bookstore on Madison Avenue. When asked what his customers were like for an article in *American Way* magazine in 1979, he sounded like he was describing Malcolm Forbes. "Toy soldier collectors think of their prized acquisitions as 'charming toys,'" he said. "They're not a bunch of guys running around rattling their sabers. Very few of the people who come into my shop have more than a passing interest in battles and campaigns. It's the color and spectacle that attracts them—the troops on parade and the marching bands."

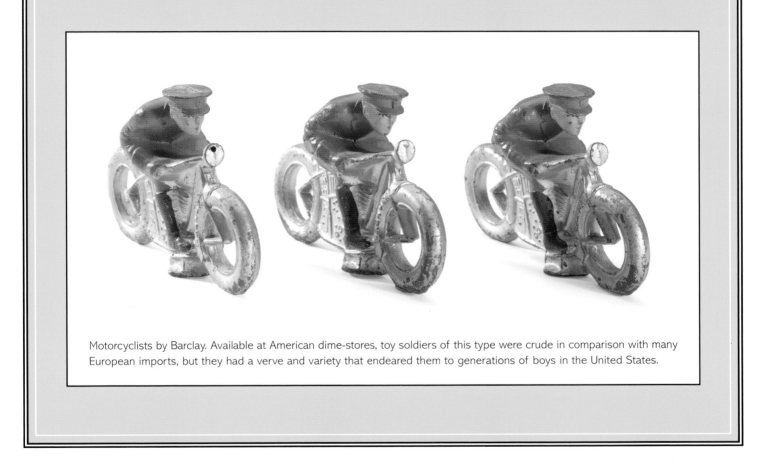

Motorcyclists by Barclay. Available at American dime-stores, toy soldiers of this type were crude in comparison with many European imports, but they had a verve and variety that endeared them to generations of boys in the United States.

The museum was the Palais Mendoub in Tangier, Morocco, where the Johnsons were co-curators. The book was *Toy Armies*, by Peter Johnson. But, before we explore how this collection was built and how these little soldiers took many a lengthy journey to new exhibits, let's examine the man who was behind it all: the wealthy and worldly Malcolm Forbes.

Incidentally, Forbes, the twice-decorated war hero, is handsomely represented in his collection. One Forbes toy soldier wears a combat-worn tunic with a label which reads, "101st General Hospital. Staff Sergeant Forbes, Malcolm S./35617834:"; there are also other soldiers wearing Forbes' Purple Heart and Bronze Star, complete with the Bronze Star citation for meritorious service in Europe in 1944.

Dreams of Glory Charles Spencelayh oil on canvas 1900 **30" x 20"**

CHAPTER 2:

MEET MALCOLM FORBES, A WORLD-CLASS COLLECTOR

"ANY GOOD COLLECTION HAS A PERSONAL SPARK
THAT GIVES IT ITS HUMAN DIMENSION."

—Malcolm Forbes

alcolm Forbes, who was born in 1919 and died in 1990, lived life to the fullest. He is best known as the man who took the magazine his father founded, *Forbes*, and transformed it into one of America's most successful business publications. Forbes once said his financial success provided the means for him to indulge his passions, including the sheer joy of accumulating one of the world's largest and most valuable collections of toy soldiers.

In addition to serving in the United States military, Forbes also served as a state senator from 1952 to 1958. He was elected in New Jersey, and he was the state's Republican candidate for governor in 1957, an election he lost.

When he wasn't in his office, he partook in many other leisure activities, including yachting and riding in his hot air balloon. Malcolm received the Harmon Trophy for Aeronaut of the Year in 1975 for setting six world hot air ballooning records. He also enjoyed touring various countries on his motorcycle and—perhaps one of his favorite hobbies—collecting.

But when did his massive army of toy soldiers begin to take shape? Why did he build such a monumental collection? And what was it that triggered this burst of nostalgia and collecting fervor?

"There were five boys in our family and all of us got into toy soldiers," Forbes said in "Malcolm Forbes: Toy Soldiers' Commander-in-Chief," *Collectibles Illustrated*, May/ June 1983. "With imagination there was no limit to what you could do with them. We used to war with each other, literally, as brothers do, but also with each others' soldiers. I'd build a castle of blocks and stick my soldiers in it. Then my oldest brother, who was a great marble player, would fire his shooter and knock down the castle." Though Forbes' father gave him very little spending money, he often did odd jobs, such as washing or mowing lawns in order to make enough money to buy the toy soldiers he adored.

ONCE HE STARTED COLLECTING TOY SOLDIERS,
FORBES COULDN'T STOP, WHETHER HE SAW THEM AT
A FLEA MARKET, AN ANTIQUE SHOP, OR AN AUCTION

ALEXANDER THE GREAT AND THE PERSIANS
The Heinrichsen firm in Nüremberg came out with this beautifully engraved and painted set depicting the 331 B.C. defeat of the Persians by Alexander the Great.

ARAB SOLDIERS

Arabs dancing with swords, made by various French manufacturers.

BIRTH OF THE LITTLE TIN SOLDIER

Bugles cry and drums roll in the imagination of a child, as rank upon rank of soldiers march into battle across a nursery shelf. And so it has been for more than 200 years. Miniature figures have been around for untold centuries, but large scale production began in the tin-rich region around Nüremberg, Germany, in the last half of the eighteenth century. Using excess metal from the production of kitchenware, pewter artisans fashioned flat, two-dimensional figures for the delight of their children. Johann Gottfried Hilpert was among the first to realize their commercial potential. By 1770 he had begun to produce hunting, farming, and wildlife figures. Soon, inspired by the military feats of Prussia's Frederick the Great, toy armies marched into the playrooms of Europe. To this day a flourishing flat industry thrives in Germany and Austria.

"When I went away to school at the age of 13," Forbes said, "I turned over my collection to my younger brother. That was the end of my playing days. Eventually, all our toy soldiers disappeared." But all those great childhood memories came bubbling to the surface when Forbes began collecting his miniature militia in the late 1960s. He was at an auction house in New York with the idea of bidding on some paintings. A couple of small lots of toy soldiers came up for bid. When Forbes saw the soldiers, they rekindled memories of his childhood. It was a set of "worse-for-wear" World War I American doughboys. "Up went my hand," he said, "and it has stayed mostly up ever since."

Once he started collecting toy soldiers, Forbes couldn't stop, whether he saw them at a flea market, an antique shop, or an auction. In the early days, Forbes focused principally on the toy soldiers made by the legendary British toy maker Britains (see Chapter 4 for profiles of the major toy soldier manufacturers). And, to this day, the Britains soldiers domi-

Men of the Yorkshire Regiment preparing for a meal. A toy soldier vignette from Harold Pestana's army, Soldiers of the Queen.

BRITAINS SOLDIERS DOMINATE THE COLLECTION IN THE
FORBES GALLERIES AND ARE THE ONES MOST SOUGHT AFTER
BY KNOWLEDGEABLE COLLECTORS

BRITAINS SOLDIERS AT CHRISTMAS
More of Pestana's Soldiers of the Queen, seen here decorating a Christmas tree.

T H E   S A C K   O F   T R O Y

Part fiction and part fact, the tale of the Trojan War was told by the blind Greek storyteller Homer in *The Iliad* and *The Odyssey*. The conflict began, legend says, after Paris, son of King Priam of Troy, kidnapped the beautiful Helen. The Greeks, led by King Agamemnon, laid siege for ten years to the city of Troy on the coast of Asia Minor. Finally they achieved victory using a ruse suggested by the hero Ulysses. Pretending to retreat, they left a large hollow wooden horse as a gift for the Trojans. Inside were Greek warriors who opened the city to their comrades and then sacked and burned the city. In this scene created by Heyde, a priest inside the walls of Troy entreats the gods who, Homer says, capriciously interfered on both sides in the war. The horse is shown with the ladder used by the Greek hero Achilles. He drags the body of Hector, the valiant Trojan he defeated in single combat, with the help of the goddess Athena.

nate the collection in the Forbes Galleries and are the ones most sought after by knowledgeable collectors.

Britains produced more toy soldiers than any other company. Its soldiers are not hard to find, but they have always been deemed the most desirable. However, as Forbes bought more and more soldiers, he began to appreciate the soldiers that came before Britains. This included two-dimensional "flats," which he had pretty much ignored in his youth. But

as he became a more knowledgeable collector, Forbes began to admire the artistry—the superb detailing and highly animated sculpting—required to make a first-rate flat.

Initially Forbes kept his toy collection in his den. But when he found himself with several thousand tiny troops, he decided to share his treasures with the public. And he had the perfect place—make that palace—to house his army.

BIRTH OF THE LITTLE TIN SOLDIER (DETAIL)

Refusing to bow down to Austrian sovereignty, the legendary fourteenth century Swiss hero, William Tell, is ordered by the Austrian governor Gessler to shoot an apple off the head of his own son with a crossbow. The tale is told in metal by the well-known German firm of Ernst Heinrichsen of Nüremberg.

Flats

Although military models can be traced back to Roman times, the toy soldiers that became a mass-market phenomenon marched out of the factories in Nüremberg, Germany, beginning in 1848 with flats. The soldiers that ruled supreme throughout most of the nineteenth century were the two-dimensional flats, and their most prominent maker was Heinrichsen, which produced soldiers just over an inch tall—known as the "Nüremberg scale." Flats were sold by weight; they ranged from the troops of military leaders like Frederick the Great and Napoleon to civilians engaged in their daily routines. The thin flats were cast from tin in molds that were engraved in slate. These flats were produced in Germany and Austria.

Semi-Rounds

Cast in solid lead, these little soldiers weren't quite three-dimensional. First made in Germany in the 1830s, they were superseded by the solid toy soldier, but they remained popular in Austria well into the twentieth century.

The earliest fully rounded metal soldiers were pioneered by Lucotte of France all the way back in 1785. Considered among the finest ever made, Lucotte figures are also among the rarest, and collectors hotly pursue them. Other makers—most notably Mignot in France and Heyde in Germany—were also known for three-dimensional soldiers that commanded high prices and appealed to the toy soldier connoisseur.

Hollow-cast Soldiers

In all of toy soldier history, the most important year was 1892. According to legend, William Britain, Jr. was whiling away the hours under a cherry tree behind his father's toy factory on Hornsey Rise in North London. He was playing with a mold and somehow got it into his head that maybe he could figure out a way to cast a better figure than anything the French or Germans had devised. Back in the factory, William discovered that with a quick flick of his wrist he could force molten lead out of the mold through holes in the soldier's head and feet. As simple as this sounds, it was a manufacturing breakthrough. Britain's invention—known as the hollow-cast soldier—obviously required far less lead than the competitors' solid figures. Priced at roughly half of what solid soldiers' cost, Britains quickly took over the market, making affordable toy soldiers. Britains quickly became the world's largest producer of toy soldiers. Still the most widely collected, the soldiers were produced right up until 1966.

Dime-Store Soldiers

Exclusively an American phenomenon, these spirited little soldiers were sold principally through five-and-ten-cents stores from the 1920s through the 1940s. Usually crafted with a hollow casting technique, some also were made of cast iron.

Paper Toy Soldiers

Made all over Europe and the United States from the late eighteenth century onward, these toy soldiers were actually printed on sheets of paper or cardboard, then cut out and mounted on blocks of wood.

Composition Soldiers

These figures are made of various materials, most commonly a mixture of sawdust and glue molded around a metal armature. Composition toy soldiers were initially manufactured in Austria at the end of the nineteenth century. Their heyday was in Germany during the 1930s and 1940s, until the end of World War II. The primary composition figures were pre-war German soldiers—including engineers, signal officers, and medical and off-duty figures. Those produced in Germany—most notably by Lineol and Elastolin—were called *masse figuren*. Composition figures also were manufactured in France, Belgium and Italy, where they were known as "pasta" figures. Composition figures are notoriously prone to damage or disintegration if stored in damp conditions. The wire armature often rusts and expands, which causes the figures to crack open.

Specialists at the Forbes Galleries go to great lengths to create an environment to minimize the deterioration. Visitors are astonished by the condition of the soldiers, many of which are more than 100 years old.

A Z T E C   P Y R A M I D

Arrayed around the Pyramid of the Sun in Tenochtitlan—today's Mexico City—Aztec warriors in feather regalia and jaguar skins battle in vain against the troops and Indian allies of Hernán Cortés in 1521. The large intricate set was produced by Aloys Ochel of Germany, the world's largest maker of flat tin figures.

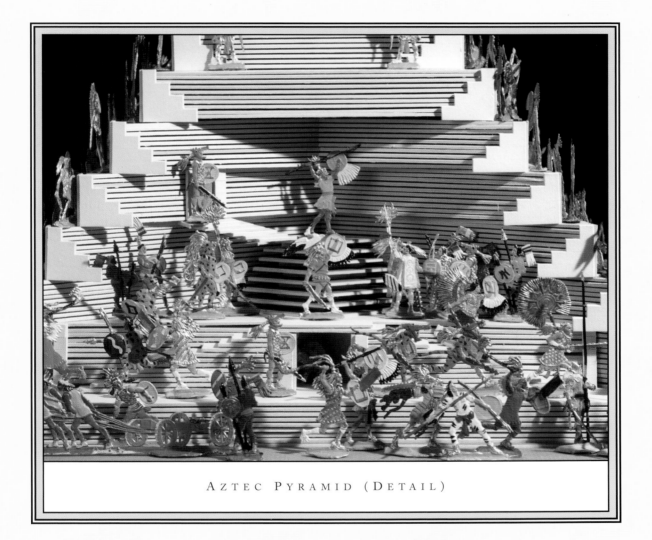

AZTEC PYRAMID (DETAIL)

COURTENAY KNIGHT

British-born Richard Courtenay, renowned for his medieval heraldic model figures, crafted this 3" knight, which bears a coat of arms with a lion rampant on his crested helmet and cloth surcoat worn over his armor. The horse wears a long flowing coat, similarly emblazoned, for protection against arrows. Note the "plug shoulder" which enables the knight to brandish his sword.

CHAPTER 3:

THE ULTIMATE ODYSSEY

"PAYMASTER, QUARTERMASTER, RECRUITING SERGEANT, AND COMMANDING GENERAL, MALCOLM FORBES IS A MAN OF ALL WARS IN ALL PLACES IN ALL TIMES."

—*The Washington Times*, **November 19, 1982**

Like every great businessman and manager, Forbes was a master of delegation. Hence, he delegated considerable responsibility for selecting the most suitable soldiers for his collection to the Johnsons.

Forbes was so impressed with the Johnsons' knowledge of toy soldiers that he made them an irresistible offer. He sent a letter to Anne Johnson asking if she and her husband would be interested in an exotic Arabian adventure, which meant traveling to the palace he owned in Morocco and building a world-beater collection.

The Johnsons spent many years as co-curators of the toy soldier collection at the Palais Mendoub on Rue Shakespeare in Tangier, which became a museum in 1978. They lived amid great beauty "here on the tip of Africa, where Mediterranean meets Atlantic and East meets West . . . ." Elizabeth Taylor used Palais Mendoub on her honeymoon with Larry Fortensky, and numerous film directors used it for scenes in movies, and it had once served as "the residence of the Mendoub, or Sultan's representative, in the days when the port was an international zone." (*Military Modelling*, 1979.)

As curators, the Johnsons made numerous trips—including to England—and they spent considerable time identifying and recommending to Forbes which toy soldiers should be acquired. When the museum officially opened, the collection comprised approximately 5,000 troops.

Although major acquisitions were usually made at auction houses—Sotheby's, Christie's, and especially Phillips in London—Forbes also purchased toy soldiers from individual collectors. He also placed ads to find them. For example, on October 20, 1978, Forbes wrote a letter to Peter Johnson proposing the following ad to run in "the most widely-read, appropriate two or three British magazines aimed at toy soldier hobbyists":

U.S. collector seeks unusual and/or rare old and very old military toy sets, dioramas, pieces for museum. Collections of any size are of interest. Please send description, photograph, prices to: Malcolm Forbes, Old Battersea House.

FRENCH AIRPORT SCENE

This airport scene was made in France and includes its original landscaped box.

A MAN CALLED BRITAIN

A name that has come to be synonymous with lead soldiers appeared in 1893 when William Britain Jr. of London invented a revolutionary hollow-cast soldier that was lighter and more economical than the continental solids. The firm grew rapidly as its cheaper soldiers conquered the toy army markets of Europe and the United States. Britains produced nearly every regiment of the British Army and hundreds from other nations. Collectors of Britains figures in the United States and Europe now outnumber all others.

One of Forbes' many properties, the Old Battersea House, was where he coordinated the buildup in his toy army.

One of the largest early acquisitions was the 1979 purchase of roughly 40,000 toy soldiers from the German Federal Republic's military history museum in Rastatt, Germany. Consisting of flats made by Kiel and other German manufacturers, this legion was so large that an addition had to be built at the Palais Mendoub museum.

The collection eventually evolved to a force exceeding 100,000 toy soldiers. *Art & Antiques Weekly* reported on a sale at the Phillips auction house on November 26, 1980. It was "a whole battalion of the London Scottish Regiment"

acquired by Forbes for £5,200, making "this battalion the most expensive toy soldiers in the world. The 666-man unit, including fighting troops and transport, represents a battalion on active service in France in 1916. The London Scottish was the first territorial regiment to take part in the war." Phillips reported that this was the most comprehensive assortment and among the most accurate and richly detailed soldiers they had ever offered at auction.

Forbes also purchased a very impressive collection from an American attorney. According to an article published in *The Post-Standard* of Syracuse, New York on November 13, 1981, "It was no regular army that Crouse Barnum accumu-

FORBES COMMISSIONED ENGINEERS TO PRODUCE SPECIAL
EFFECTS LIKE HOOFBEATS, MARTIAL MUSIC, THE SOUND
OF BATTLEFIELD WEAPONS AND ARTILLERY

A MAN CALLED BRITAIN (DETAIL):
AIR DEFENSE

lated quietly in Syracuse when he first began playing with toy soldiers . . . in the 1920s." As Peter Johnson said in a letter to Malcolm Forbes, it was a rare collection the late Barnum's family sold to Malcolm Forbes.

Robert Forbes, who helped his father build the toy soldiers collection, said Barnum's was "a very high-quality collection" and that he and Forbes "were impressed and surprised" to come across it. Robert said the Barnum collec-

bomber circa 1938, by Tippco.

Phillips had estimated the field medical unit would sell for £1,500 to £2,000 (far less than the winning bid of £2,800) and that the monoplane bomber would command £300 to £400. But Peter Johnson was thrilled. He felt that the medical unit was worth about twice what he paid and the monoplane was a wonderful complement to the rest of the German military hardware in the Forbes collection. In fact,

MEDICS AT THE FRONT LINE

The toy makers of Germany and Britain excelled at creating realistic units of medical field personnel. Scarlet ambulance wagons roll past medics tending the wounded in a superb and rare set piece of the late nineteenth century by Heyde.

tion—for which Forbes paid $40,000—"is one of the best they have in their possession. Among the most precious were medieval knights with removable helmets and movable lance arms."

Other significant toy soldiers (also purchased at a Phillips auction) were from a collection of 22,000 soldiers accumulated by John Hanington, a British surgeon. Peter Johnson attended this auction on behalf of Forbes. The tented British Army field hospital circa 1910 cost £2,800, and Forbes paid £2,200 for a monoplane clockwork dive-

in a letter to Margaret Kelly (now Margaret Trombly), Vice President of the Forbes Collection, prior to the auction, Johnson said the medical field hospital was "the star lot of the sale . . . never been seen before . . . a most desirable piece which could go well above" Phillips' estimate. (See Chapter 5 for a full analysis of the toy soldier as an investment.)

Whatever the Forbes family paid for their beloved soldiers, they were confident the collection was worth far more than they paid. And people were awestruck, a reaction that satisfied Forbes.

A MAN CALLED BRITAIN (DETAIL)

The Royal State Coach for the coronation of King George V is the focus in the castle courtyard, while battalions of the Household Cavalry Band and the Life Guards add to the festivities. Manufactured by William Britain Jr. of London, his firm produced nearly every regiment of the British Army, as well as hundreds from other nations.

Forbes wanted his collection to be as dramatic and entertaining as possible. He commissioned engineers to produce special effects like hoofbeats, martial music, the sound of battlefield weapons and artillery. Visitors to the galleries in New York often remark on the lifelike exhibits; they make history come to life before their very eyes and ears.

In the winter of 1984, after roughly 10,000 of the Forbes toy soldiers were moved into the Forbes Galleries in New York, Peter Johnson filed one of his periodic toy soldier reviews for Forbes. In this report, Johnson commented that the first floor of the *Forbes* magazine building on Fifth Avenue had undergone a year-long transformation to accommodate the Forbes collections.

This report celebrated the Forbes toy soldiers collection in New York City, which appealed to almost everyone—the casual observer, the novice collector, the history lover, and the serious collector—from the early flats to the semi-solids, the solids, the Britains hollow-casts, the German compositions, up to the dime-store toy soldiers.

In one panorama, George Washington's troops appear to be on the move, and some of the most famous (and infamous) figures in history—William Tell, Buffalo Bill, Queen Victoria, King George V, and Queen Mary—are represented. There are nineteenth-century field hospitals, sailors and ships. But words alone cannot describe this exhibit. Only first-hand observation in the Forbes Galleries can do it justice.

When you visit the Forbes toy soldiers collection, you will see the rare sets of toy soldiers crafted by Heyde. You will see William Britain's finest creations—including the Village Idiot—in a castle dominating an entire wall. And you will see the ingenious work of designers Peter Purpura and Gary Kisner, including a little boy's bedroom in *Land of Counterpane*.

FRANCE ENTERS THE ARENA

Inspired by the victories of Napoleon, the French plunged into the design and manufacture of elaborate solid figures with a vengeance. The legions of the Grande Armée marched from the firm of Mignot of Paris. From marshals to drummers, uniforms were accurate to the last detail. Older figures of Mignot and its predecessor, Lucotte, are today among the most valuable toy soldiers in the world. Although the French excelled in quality, Heyde retained its following with extraordinary creations, such as the rare drum carriage of the Elector of Saxony and the British coronation coach.

FRANCE ENTERS THE ARENA

Rank and file parade in an original landscaped box in this rare and valuable set of flats by Mignot. Only 20 mm tall, the 1,400 pieces represent French infantry, cavalry, and artillery in the Franco-Prussian War of 1870. A Phillips news release dated March 1980 made this report: "A Mignot: Large 1400 figure of French Infantry, Artillery and Cavalry Regiments advancing in the Franco-Prussian war (lot 321) sold for $1,500 surpassing its estimate of $600/900."

GUARDSMAN ON HORSEBACK WITH RAISED SWORD

FORBES SOLDIERS SHOWCASED IN
NATIONAL GEOGRAPHIC SOCIETY EXHIBITION

In December 1982, a sizeable contingent of the Forbes toy soldiers collection invaded the nation's capital. On December 2, *The Weekly Navy News* sounded the alarm: "The headquarters building of the National Geographic Society . . . has recently become the encampment of some 12,000 military men and women from around the world—as well as many from several centuries ago."

The Navy publication was referring to an exhibition entitled *On Parade: A Pageant of Toy Soldiers*, at the National Geographic Society's Explorers Hall, which attracted hundreds of thousands of visitors.

In an article appearing in at least half a dozen newspapers, Daniel P. Jones captured the essence of the National Geographic exhibit. "As much as the exhibit in Washington stokes the coals of one's imagination, it warmly evokes the memories of youth, rainy afternoons or sick days home from school setting up battles on bedroom floors."

WASHINGTON REVIEWS HIS TROOPS

In all the splendor of their 1776 uniforms, the Revolutionary War troops of the original Thirteen Colonies march past their leader, General George Washington. These modern, solid figures were made by Richards Soldiers of Scarsdale, NY.

WASHINGTON REVIEWS HIS TROOPS (DETAIL)

On parade are the flags and units of Massachusetts, New Hampshire, Rhode Island, Connecticut, New York, New Jersey, Pennsylvania, Delaware, Maryland, Virginia, North Carolina, South Carolina, and Georgia. Reviewing the parade, Washington is flanked by a guard of Continental Marines (which became the United States Marine Corps) and backed by the muzzle-loading artillery of his army.

The Forbes toy soldiers collection includes some masterful dioramas by Harold Pestana, who was associate professor of geology at Colby College in Waterville, Maine. After seeing the Forbes toy soldiers exhibit at the National Geographic Society, Mr. Pestana wrote a brief note to Forbes: "What a lovely and fantastic display it makes and it is really nice of you to share your 'troops' with the public. I was impressed not only by the displays, but also by the uniformly positive comments made by the people viewing the cases. It was nice to see so many of my old regiments performing as they were intended to."

ANDREW WYETH ON TOY SOLDIERS

A charming letter from the painter Andrew Wyeth, in which he thanks friends for a gift of miniature Revolutionary War soldiers. He writes: "Now I must get paint and do a job on them."

CHAPTER 4:

GIANTS WALKED THE TOY SOLDIER BATTLEFIELD

"AS ANY MAN, OF ANY AGE, WILL TELL YOU, IT'S FUN PLAYING WITH TOY SOLDIERS."

—Peter Johnson, *Smithsonian*, 1980

The Forbes toy soldiers collection is distinguished by its rich variety of forms—from the old two-dimensional flat figures to the hollow soldiers pioneered by the British firm of Britains.

Here are biographies of the designers and manufacturers who created the collection at the Forbes Galleries in New York City.

HILPERT

Johann Gottfried Hilpert was born in 1732. After studying to be a pewter artisan in his hometown of Coburg in southern Germany, Hilpert moved south to the larger and more vibrant city of Nüremberg to continue his apprenticeship. There, in 1760, at the age of 28, he became a master tinsmith. Europe was embroiled in the Seven Years War, and Hilpert began to make silver models of soldiers. By 1770 he was well known for the quality of his flat figures. Hilpert's business ultimately became a family affair when his brother Johann Georg and his son Johann Wolfgang joined the business. However, when Johann Gottfried died in 1801, his molds were sold and the Hilpert soldiers diminished in quality. Today the original Hilpert soldiers are so rare that few collectors have ever seen one unless, of course, they visit the Forbes Galleries.

HEINRICHSEN

Johann Gottfried Hilpert influenced many fine German toy makers, most notably Ernst Heinrichsen. Perhaps Heinrichsen's greatest contribution to toy soldiers was to standardize them. In 1848, he introduced and sold the 30mm figure in large quantities; this size became known as the "Nüremberg scale." This was a very important development because shops could display many manufacturers' soldiers together.

"With demand for tin figures growing in the nineteenth

THE FORBES TOY SOLDIER COLLECTION IS

DISTINGUISHED BY ITS RICH VARIETY OF FORMS

DRESDEN DELIGHTS

George Heyde of Dresden was the king of the German solids. His firm flourished from the end of the Franco-Prussian War until it was destroyed in the bombing of Dresden in World War II. Though sometimes lacking in historical accuracy, Heyde's figures were rich in variety and style, and the firm's soldiers and civilian figures delighted millions of children on both sides of the Atlantic. There were innumerable parade and battle figures, but some of Heyde's most sensational stars were the special sets depicted here and elsewhere in the Forbes Galleries.

D R E S D E N   D E L I G H T S   (D E T A I L)

Disaster struck Ethiopia in 1935 when, at the direction of Benito Mussolini, the Italians invaded the North African nation. Poorly trained and ill-equipped, the Ethiopians soon succumbed to the Europeans.

Dignitaries and foreign representatives attend the 1889 coronation of Menelik II, Emperor of Ethiopia, who laid the foundations for his country's emergence as a modern state.

century, Nüremberg craftsmen looked for ways to mass-produce them more economically," said to John Dornberg in *Museum* magazine. For almost a century, the shop created more than 17,000 different molds and millions of figures. "There was hardly a child in Europe who didn't have Heinrichsen miniatures in the toy box. And the themes of the series covered every aspect of human activity and history in both war and peace."

BRITAINS

Britains has been called the greatest family business in the history of toys. The founder, William Britain (1826–1906) was a true entrepreneur, blessed with creativity, vitality, and a fervent belief in the free enterprise system. He also had the good fortune of being born with a last name that provided a powerful brand in Great Britain. Moreover, his children shared his work ethic and his love of toys.

In 1892, William Britain Jr. figured out how to make lead soldiers hollow on the inside. They were cheaper to manufacture so Britains was able to dominate the market. About two-thirds of the several billion lead soldiers in the world created between 1895 and 1965 have come from Britains.

William Britain left his factory to his first child, Emily, when he died. Her brothers bought her out. William Jr. came up with the idea of the hollow-cast lead soldier that took over the market of the toy soldier. Brother Alfred became the firm's managing director and brother Fred was a salesman and the company secretary.

FLAT SOLDIERS ARE NOT SO FLAT

While many collectors used to consider the flat two-dimensional soldiers inferior to the hollow-cast or solid three-dimensional figures, the most knowledgeable authorities on the topic seem to have a special fondness for the flat figures, especially the earliest ones. Heinrichsen and Aloys Ochel not only bring the armies of ancient history to life, but they also depict scenes of peace and tranquility. They include the simple life enjoyed by people in small towns and rural communities, as well as the drama of operas and theatrical events and the grandeur of coronations, fêtes, and historical pageants.

The techniques used to craft flats were always the same. They were characteristically cast from a mold of two closely adhering slabs of shale, slate, or schist into which the front and back sides of a master image had been engraved. However simple it seems, the process was "in fact a painstaking and time-consuming handicraft demanding not only much patience but, above all, great artistry and skill on the part of the engraver," art historian John Dornberg noted in *Museum* magazine in 1982. "Those early Nüremberg tin and lead craftsmen called their shops offinen, offocinas. The term, once used for apothecaries, alluded to their mastery of chemical and metallurgical secrets and the mysteries of alloy smelting."

These figures evolved from "rough replicas into little works of art, thanks to talented engravers who, in the manner of silversmiths, impressed each of their miniatures with signatures and hallmarks," Dornberg said.

Dornberg observed the early German flat soldier makers were as skilled at marketing and sales as they were in making toys. By the seventeenth century they were exporting their little metal toys to children throughout Europe. By the nineteenth century, the soldiers of Nüremberg enlivened the homes of many children from the middle and mercantile classes.

IN THE NAPOLEONIC TRADITION OF PRODUCING
SPLENDID ARMIES, FRENCH TOY MAKERS HAVE
PRODUCED THE FINEST TOY SOLDIERS

HEYDE

Heyde of Dresden is by far the best known German manufacturer of solid toy soldiers, and the Heyde company dominated the lead toy soldier arena in the late nineteenth century. The factory was destroyed by Allied bombs in 1945. Heyde figures were solid and very animated, with plenty of hand-painted details. Heyde did not craft soldiers to a standard scale and frequently enhanced its creations with attachments of soft lead. These embellishments were fragile and easily broken.

Heyde competed aggressively with manufacturers in France. But experts have observed that Heyde soldiers were often lacking in historical accuracy. For example, the company would use the same molds to produce the cavalry and infantry of different nations, the only distinction being the color of the uniforms. However, Heyde won high marks for creating a rich variety of poses and tableau. This was in contrast to firms like Britain, which produced the usual marching, standing, riding, firing, and charging soldiers. Peter Johnson observed in "A Heyde Tiger Hunt for Christmas," published in *Antique Finder*, November 1979, "Heyde lancers relaxed in bivouac, playing cards, drinking schnapps and washing shirts; signalers erected telegraph poles and pioneers built bridges; flying aces tended aircraft engines and sailors swabbed decks. But the stuff of Christmas presents were the delightful 'civvy' sets, which explored the romance of tiger hunting in India, buffalo shoots in the Wild West and even the magic of fairy tales."

TOY SOLDIERS PUT ON WEIGHT

The flat soldier was remarkable for the detail on the one-millimeter-thick figures, but it seemed only a natural progression to begin to make them more lifelike. In Germany, toy soldier manufacturers produced a transitional semi-flat of ten millimeters thickness, but these hybrids soon faded from fashion as full rounds came into vogue. About the time of the French Revolution of 1789, solid and more expensive figures of lead and antimony began to appear in France. The casts were made from bronze moulds engraved with elaborate detail. *The Sham Fight*, (at far right) a set of flats, was produced for the English market by the German firm of Heyde. Opposing forces were aligned at equal distances from one another. Taking turns, commanders fired a cannon armed with a pea, scoring points for knockdowns: private – 1, drummer – 2, sergeant – 4, captain – 8. Vanquishing a colonel counted for 10 points and an automatic win.

MIGNOT

In the Napoleonic tradition of producing splendid armies, French toy makers have produced the finest toy soldiers. The oldest French toy soldier maker still in existence—Mignot—made fully round, three-dimensional solid metal figures. Some of the company's old brass molds are still in use. Older Mignot sets are highly prized by collectors. The Napoleonics and Ancients are particularly popular.

LINEOL

Lineol produced toy figures based on goose-stepping Nazi soldiers, delighting both the Führer and a legion of German children. Just as Adolf Hitler's troops "took on a more offensive, attacking posture, closer in spirit to the Third Reich's expansionist aims, Lineol took up the challenge with gusto. And its new range of skillfully modeled figures, equipped with all the firepower and support equipment its designers could create, temporarily grabbed the lead from Elastolin." What followed was an arms race between two toy-making superpowers. Some of the vehicles were so true to life that "the Wehrmacht's own security people had to step in and

veto a detail still on the secret list . . ." (*Old Toy Soldier Newsletter*, December 1979.)

Lineol was known for its highly realistic composition figures. Now owned by Gert Duscha, who bought the company in 1980, Lineol still casts resin figures with the original molds, as well as manufacturing a full line of new figures and accessories. These figures are meticulously detailed and painted by hand. They are produced in small quantities, assuring their future rarity.

ELASTOLIN

Elastolin wasn't a company, but a brand name. The company was O & M Hausser, best known for creating figures of Nazi leaders and other military models during the Third Reich. In addition to toy soldiers, Hausser mass-produced trenches, command posts, field hospitals, shell dumps, and every detail of the carnage of World War I. Elastolin accessories were made from heavy pressed tin. Derived from the craft of the medieval Bavarian woodcarver, Elastolin figures were made of a wire-reinforced composition of casein glue and sawdust forced into a mold.

Before World War II, Elastolin's biggest market was

Great Britain. While its figures were a bit pricey, they still found a receptive audience. The Elastolin figures actually looked like antiques. The horses were unmatched in texture and color. Their red-rimmed eyes, tossing manes and beautifully painted accoutrements made them especially attractive.

Elastolin was founded in Neustadt, in northern Franconia in the former kingdom of Bavaria. However, toward the end of World War II, the Elastolin factory at Neustadt was destroyed. After the war, production resumed but no war toys were made. Instead, Elastolin created cowboys and Indians that were among the brand's best works.

ALOYS OCHEL

After World War I, a German association of collectors formed a company called Fabrik fur Kulturhistorische Zinn-figuren und Kulturbilder GmbH Kiel. Aloys Ochel of Kiel, Germany acquired this company. Relying on the talents of such master engravers as Ludwig Frank, Aloys Ochel elevated the flat to the stature of a work of art. According to the *Old Toy Soldier Newsletter*, December 1979, "When expertly painted, flats by Ochel are exquisite creations, fully justifying the argument from enthusiasts of flats that the artistry . . . surpassing anything that can be achieved by the maker of a semi or full-round figure."

MANOIL

In 1928, Jack and Maurice Manoil started Man-O-Lamp Corporation in New York. It is not known precisely when they started making toy soldiers (probably in 1935), but we do know their first soldier was No. 7 Flag Bearer. "The initial

TOY SOLDIERS PUT ON WEIGHT (DETAIL)

A landing party of American sailors takes the beach in this naval tableau, a semi-round creation by an unknown German firm.

TOY SOLDIERS PUT ON WEIGHT (DETAIL)

Kaiser William II, Emperor of Germany and King of Prussia, with his wife, the Kaiserin, review troops prior to World War I. This semi-round set is the work of Heyde of Dresden.

line of figures was a blend of cowboys, Indians, sailors, and soldiers, but as the line expanded it became purely military." (*The World Encyclopedia of Model Soldiers*, 1981.) Manoil appealed to dime-store patrons. Like most dime-store figures, these American soldiers—wearing tin hats and carrying flags—were purchased individually.

The figures were sculpted in clay, then plaster molds were made and the figures were cast in bronze. The bronze mold was "fitted with an ejector and mounted in an adjustable steel cradle. The cradle had a built-in lever which allowed the mold to open and close. When opened all the way, the ejector would be engaged, leaving the casting suspended between the mold halves. The cradle swiveled on posts, allowing the mold to be inverted. With this efficient device, a master and his assistant could turn out hundreds of castings daily." (*The World Encyclopedia of Model Soldiers*, 1981.) These innovative techniques, along with improved molds, enabled Manoil to be highly competitive. However, metal became very scarce during World War II and Manoil

ceased operations on April 1, 1942. After the war Manoil made mostly plastic soldiers. Metal again grew scarce during the Korean War, and Manoil Manufacturing Company folded in 1953.

DURSO

A number of smaller firms worked in the shadow of the prominent German firms. One of these was Durso of Belgium, which created Native American figures, new at the Forbes Galleries, as well as portrait figures of Stalin and Charles de Gaulle.

NOSTALGIA

Shamus Wade, a British collector, was the creator of Nostalgia toy soldiers. Unlike other manufacturers, whose figures were differentiated only by the uniform of their country, Wade's philosophy was to discover the man first, then add

the uniform. His Nostalgia troops, depicting soldiers of the British Empire from 1850 and 1910, were well received.

PESTANA SOLDIERS OF THE QUEEN

Harold Pestana was a professor of geology at Colby College in Maine who spent eight years capturing the essence of British Victorian military life in toy soldiers. Beginning in 1972, he created a unique army of about 1,500 figures that had the same spirit and charm as Britain's lead figures. As Victoria's army grew, the professor decided to call his series

Soldiers of the Queen and house them in red boxes. In *Toy Armies*, Pestana said, "I got Mr. William Miller of the Colby College art department to design a box label for me. The Queen's picture on the label comes from the label on Bombay Gin." In 1980 the Forbes Museum of Military Miniatures acquired Pestana's collection.

DISCOVERY OF THE NORTH POLE

This unique set of tin flats made in Germany commemorates the American discovery of the North Pole by Robert E. Peary on April 6, 1909. Flats, the earliest tin figures, were crafted by pewtersmiths from metal scraps beginning in Germany in the late eighteenth century. These two-dimensional figures were hand-engraved and hand-painted to realistically depict actual historic moments such as the famous Arctic journey.

MANY SOLDIERS WERE PAINTED BY WOMEN IN THEIR HOMES

The process of crafting flat soldiers involved hand painting engraved blanks. The wives of farmers near Nüremberg carried out this work. About once a week, company representatives would visit the farms, drop off new patterns and blanks, and pick up the ones that had been painted. The pay was low, but the soldiers were cheap as well. Heinrichsen tin figures were sold by weight in eighth-pound, quarter-pound, half-pound, and pound packages. Around 1900 an eighth-pound box, which would contain twenty infantrymen or ten cavalry soldiers, cost between twenty and thirty pfennigs (between five and ten cents).

This tradition of farming out the hand painting of toy soldiers was by no means unique to German manufacturers. Many other European companies followed the same practice, including Britains. Hand painting at Britains was done in the factory until after World War II, when one woman (the best Britains painter) got married and quit. She asked if she could work at home and the firm obliged. Soon Britains employed thousands of women and girls to hand-paint their soldiers.

COMPANIES COMPETE IN THE TOY SOLDIER ARENA

Long before collectors transformed playthings into collectibles, toy soldiers companies engaged in fierce competition. And, as you might expect, the battle cry was usually nationalistic. The German makers of flat figures dominated the field for nearly a hundred years. Then the solid figures of France became the rage in the nineteenth century. Then, in the nineteenth century, Britains turned the tables on France with their hollow-cast figures. The Americans were slow to enter the business, even though the United States was a fertile market for foreign toy soldiers.

Toy soldiers often reflected current events. Although the majority of Britains' soldiers were British army, in 1905 the Russo-Japanese War inspired militaristic toys. In 1916, children could pretend they were dispatching General Pershing and the U.S. Army to pursue Pancho Villa into Mexico. And it was not long after Mussolini invaded Ethiopia in 1936 when Britains created the Italian expeditionary force.

Today, these very soldiers can be seen at the Forbes Galleries.

FAMED FRONTIERSMAN BUFFALO BILL CODY

CHAPTER 5:

COLLECT FOR FUN OR INVESTMENT?

"IF YOU EVER DOUBTED THE VALUE OF
A LONG-TERM INVESTMENT PHILOSOPHY,
GO BACK TO YOUR CHILDHOOD."

—**Merrill Lynch ad, 1991**

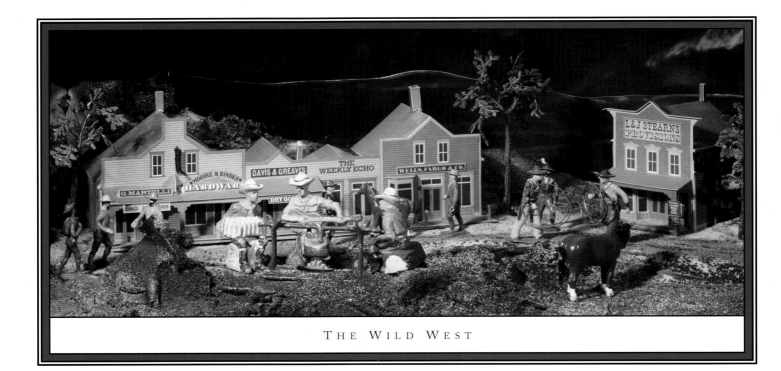

SOTHEBY'S, CHRISTIE'S, AND PHILLIPS HOLD REGULAR

SOLDIER AUCTIONS IN LONDON AND NEW YORK

The Merrill Lynch ad showed a number of toys that had appreciated dramatically over the years. Two of them were from the Forbes Galleries and one was a 1950 knight valued at $1,000. Forbes often said his motivation for collecting toy soldiers was "purely youthful memories of the fun I had with lead soldiers." But, when you consider his timing, he must have had at least one other motive.

"After the war when they stopped making the kind I'd remembered, when everything became plastic I bought a few I saw occasionally in antique stores and took them home to my four sons and my daughter. When I began to see more and more in stores I thought: 'Well, we'd better hang on to them." (*Now!*, 1979.)

In 1983, *The New York Times* said: "Collectors say part of the increased popularity of the hobby can be traced to the owner of the world's largest collection of toy soldiers, Malcolm S. Forbes, the publisher." And, a couple years earlier,

House & Garden reported Forbes had "recently at auction at Phillips in London . . . added to his collection a vintage 1916 battalion. This set of 666 soldiers of the London Scottish Regiment went to Forbes for $12,339, making it the most expensive ever auctioned."

Forbes once said he could justify his enthusiasm for collecting toy soldiers to his wife by pointing out that they are a good investment. He would persuade her of this by buying a whole lot of toy soldiers, which pushes up the price, showing her they were a good investment by their increased value.

One sign some item is hot in the collecting world is when the auction houses begin to feature it. Examples abound of record prices paid for toy soldiers in the 1980s and 1990s. One example is a set made by Britains reported by Peter Johnson in London's *Sunday Times* on January 5, 1997. "In the 1960s a boxed set of Drums and Bugles of the Line dating from the 1920s, was in great demand. The set consists

WHAT IS THE STATE OF LEAD SOLDIER COLLECTING?

by Tara Ana Finley, Independent Appraiser

Things have really changed since the early 1970s, when we saw the closet collectors come out of hiding and start to collect at major auction houses. In addition to the few newsletters and the shows, we now have the Internet, which has really changed the hobby. Collectors can now trade more freely between one another. The Internet has brought the collectors and collections much closer. Trade shows are not as popular today as they once were.

What is most desirable? One-owner collections containing rare items are still selling well. Examples would be the Bill Miele and Arnold Rolak collections, which were sold recently at auction.

Due to the cost of doing business here in the States, most major auctions of lead soldiers take place in the United Kingdom. Printing and manpower cost less there, and the collectors love any excuse to visit London.

Today, collectors are more knowledgeable, and thus rarity and provenance are extremely important. The run-of-the-mill Britain has leveled off and can be purchased over the Internet. *The Old Toy Soldier Newsletter* is now owned by one of the major dealers in the hobby. Articles about rare figures are still featured. The rare soldiers that were made by Mignot and Heyde, as well as those manufactured by William Courtenay and Des Fontaines, still make a buzz.

Tara Ana Finley has worked with Christie's, Phillips, and Doyle's auction houses as a toy soldier expert and is now an independent appraiser in Coral Gables, Florida. She has been featured on Antiques Road Show.

ARE YOU A TOY SOLDIER COLLECTOR?

Should you come across an old toy soldier in your attic or at a garage sale or flea market, there may be a few clues to its value. First, it should be stamped with the manufacturer's name. If it is in its original box—particularly if the packaging is in good shape—this can dramatically enhance its value. If it's been badly restored, this will probably diminish its value.

Beginning in the early 1980s and building right through the 1990s, other manufacturers besides Britains began to gain favor. "Of the figures most commonly available . . . Mignot, Heyde and the German composition figures made by Elastolin and Lineol demand the highest prices. Dime-store figures are usually less expensive unless found in one of the rarer forms. In all cases the collector is looking for unbroken pieces with relatively good paint condition. Soldiers with broken parts or scratched paint, unless they are rare . . . are worth little or nothing to the serious collector. In the case of composition figures, few are found without at least a few hairline cracks and, if these are not serious cracks, they will not reduce the value. In all cases, boxed sets in mint condition are the most desirable." (*Tri-State Trader*, 1982.)

Michael Goodman captures the essence of collecting in "Tin Toys and Tin Soldiers" in *Diversion* magazine in 1982: "The most important criteria in shopping for toy soldiers are rarity and condition. Minute differences between two soldiers—a helmet of unusual colors, a raised gun, an original box—determine relative values. New collectors should start with a dealer who specializes in military collectibles and toys." The dealer advises neophytes before they start bidding to attend auctions and learn firsthand what experienced collectors are avidly seeking.

THE WILD WEST (DETAIL)

Indians of similar origin demonstrate the versatility of design achieved in sawdust, glue and linseed oil composition of the 1930s and in post World War II plastic.

of seven figures, four of them modeled as boy musicians in a line regiment. You could have bought it then for £6 to £10. The price now in similar good condition would be about £350 to £400, and could rise to £500."

In 1986 in *Connoisseur* magazine, Bruce Porter said, "The fact is that in the last five years the economics of toy-soldier collecting has reached such heights that a once-playful hobby has become a serious enterprise. Sotheby's, Christie's, and

Phillips hold regular soldier auctions in London and New York, where overflow crowds of bidders, 99 percent of them adult males, vie for the little lead figures with a determination as fierce as that of any dedicated art collector. As prices for the soldiers rise, collectors are entering the field who care for the figures less as military totems than as metal objects of considerable value."

But Russell Fornwalt probably summed up the senti-

THE WILD WEST (DETAIL)
Cowboys are seen singing songs while sitting around the campfire.

Serious collectors pay attention to these conditions:

M Mint condition figures may never have been removed from their original boxes.

E Excellent figures with no obvious defects or paint chipping.

G Good figures with minimal scratches.

F Fair figures with some paint damage, but not much.

P Poor figures that need repainting and/or restoration.

Here is how the experts differentiate packaging:

E Excellent original box with no damage and all interior fittings intact.

G Good box with normal wear; some fittings may be missing.

F Fair box, may be slightly torn or split.

P Poor box, torn or split and clearly in need of repair.

Incidentally, if you see gray powder on the surface of a soldier, this is probably lead rot, a condition that has afflicted many a toy troop. It is the result of a chemical reaction, often triggered by dampness and lack of good air circulation. Soldiers with lead rot can be restored and there are ways to prevent lead rot for soldiers in your collection.

THE WILD WEST (DETAIL)

Famed frontiersman Buffalo Bill Cody watches as the Deadwood stage encounters bandits. Fortunately, a posse is on its way from town to the rescue.

THE WILD WEST (DETAIL)

Cowboys and Indians are particularly popular among toy soldiers collectors. Viewed against the backdrop of Forbes' Trinchera Ranch in Colorado, miniature braves battle settlers. The cavalry is a bugle call away. Bandits rob the stage and chiefs smoke pipes around their campfire.

Covered wagons form a protective ring against circling Sioux and Cheyenne. But rescue comes in the last reel from a troop of U.S. Cavalry. Meanwhile, somewhere north of the border, the Mounties—Royal Canadian Mounted Police—are on patrol. This classic Western scene comes to life with lead figures made by the legendary Britain.

FOR THE SERIOUS COLLECTOR, TOY SOLDIERS ARE MUCH MORE THAN PLAYTHINGS

ments of most collectors in his article in the *Tri-State Trader* in 1982, when he said: "For the serious collector, toy soldiers are much more than playthings. They are at once reminders of military history, works of art, marvels in design and manufacturing, decorative objects, conversation pieces, definitive studies in the evolution of miniatures, and pieces possessing profitable investment-potential."

What is the current climate for toy soldiers as investments? "Like many collectibles, toy soldiers grew in value steadily through the 1980s and 1990s and have now stablilized," says Richard Walker, owner of Forward March, a contemporary manufacturer of hand-painted lead soldiers. "What will happen in the future is anyone's guess."

For that reason, if you are collecting toy soldiers, it's probably best to take Forbes' advice: "If anyone should seek my advice about collecting, I'd quickly point out the old truth—buy only what you like. Measure a work by the joy and satisfaction it will bring."

THE WILD WEST

A classic Western scenario created by lead figures made by Britains for export to the American market. Reflecting an emphasis on less militaristic toys after World War I, this set depicts a wagon train surrounded by Sioux and Cheyenne Indians, while troops come to their rescue.

FORBES TRINCHERA RANCH

A cowboy riding off to the Forbes Trinchera Ranch in Colorado.

AN INTERVIEW
WITH ROBERT L. FORBES

Q. How did you decide which toy soldiers would be in the Forbes Galleries in New York?

A. Peter and Anne Johnson along with my father decided. The galleries exhibit was based directly on the display at the National Geographic that Peter Purpura and Gary Kisner put together.

Q. What became of the soldiers in Tangier, Morocco that didn't end up in New York?

A. The Tangier collection was sold many years ago. While there are some exhibits [in Tangier] that I enjoyed visiting, they are now gone. Some of the parades of soldiers and the castles full of figures were great fun, but I rely on photos to remind me of the ambience they all created at the museum.

Q. What is the current state of the toy soldier collecting arena? Have rare soldiers continued to rise in value? Would you say the Forbes collection is worth more or less than, say, ten years ago?

A. I don't really have the expertise in this area to know how the value has changed over ten years but I would strongly suspect that they have risen, in keeping with the increase in value of all good antique toys.

Q. What are your favorites in the gallery?

A. I enjoy those made by William Britain, as these remind me directly of my childhood. My dad one Christmas gave the three of us older boys full sets of soldiers, and had the helmets of two of the armies painted so we could tell whose was whose. None survive to my knowledge, though they were certainly played with a lot while we had them.

Q. What are your least favorite?

A. I find I am less drawn to the civilian models, the farms and town sets that were made after the First War in deference to the desire for things less military. As a young lad, I was more attracted to the soldiers that reminded me of my father, and what he did in the war.

Q. How would you describe the impact the Johnsons had on the collection? What percentage of the collection would you say they recommended or simply acquired for you?

A. Though my father had fun in the beginning of the collection, he was happy to let these experts do a lot of the legwork for him. They would bring him recommendations before a sale and together they would work out the parameters of purchase, where they would go and, based on the rarity, what would be a reasonable price ceiling.

Q. Which acquisitions were particularly satisfying for you?

A. I actually bought some of the ones that are in the galleries today. When my father and I were in Russia on our motorcycle trip in 1979, I bought some lead soldiers and a small set of plastic ones that I intended to give to my son. When my father saw them, he was very anxious to have them for the collection, so I happily gave them to him. Though they look quite strange, they fit in well, as reminders that there are little boys everywhere who like to play with such things.

Q. What are the most valuable soldiers in the collection?

A. As far as I know, the most valuable ones are those by Richard Courtenay, made by hand in Great Britain, depicting knights on horseback, with ladies and gentlemen in attendance, and with the king and queen to observe the jousts. The detailing is very fine and I know there were very few made.

Q. Did the Forbes Collection effectively redefine toy soldier values?

A. Up to the time of the sale, prices were holding well. At the sale itself, prices went very well for most of the pieces and sets we sold. While I would attribute lots of the strong prices to the fact that the soldiers had a fine provenance that can and often does give extra value, I would not be able to say whether the collection redefined toy soldier value.

Q. How many people visit the galleries and see the toy soldiers each year?

A. There are about 60,000 visitors a year to the galleries. While they may come to see certain exhibits, once they start to tour through, they see the soldiers and are stunned by the fullness and quality of not only the collection, but also how they are all displayed. They are not just lined up on shelves, but put into a context, with panels to explain their history.

Q. Do the soldiers still have deep personal meaning for you?

A. The soldiers do indeed still draw me in to the world they create. Some of that attraction is due to the connection they represent with my father and his enthusiasm for them. On their own, I like them for their sense of history and the stories they tell, directly by what they depict and indirectly by the manufacturers and the methods used in their production.

Richard Scholl has been a consultant, an award-winning creative director, and an author who has written about collectibles and the industry for decades. He is the author of *Matchbox Official 50th Anniversary Edition* (2002), a comprehensive pictorial history book that received rave reviews internationally. Scholl has written numerous articles on collecting and was managing editor of *The Matchbox Collector*, a newsletter published by Matchbox Collectibles for many years. Scholl worked at the Franklin Mint for several years and has since developed advertising and reference material for many of America's most prominent direct marketers of collectibles, including the Hamilton Collection, Lenox, Bradford Exchange, Action Performance, Ashton-Drake Galleries, Corgi Classics, Disney, and America Remembers. Scholl also has worked for toy companies including Tyco Preschool and Tyco R/C. A published poet, Scholl is the author of *The Running Press Glossary of Baseball Language* and has been a research consultant and contributor to many other books published by Running Press. An adjunct professor of communications at Drexel University in Philadelphia for 19 years and, more recently, professor at West Chester University in West Chester, Pa., Scholl is president of the Scholl Group, a full service advertising, communications, and marketing firm. He earned his bachelor of arts degree in writing and his master's degree in English from the Pennsylvania State University. Born in Pittsburgh, Pa., Scholl now resides in Bryn Mawr, Pa., with his wife, Catherine, and their two children, Geoffrey and Jennifer. He has also recently written another book celebrating the world's most impressive collection of toy boats, housed in the same place where the most splendid collection of toy soldiers is on display—the Forbes Galleries in New York City.

BIBLIOGRAPHY

Chelminski, Rudolph, "Forbes Museum's Little Soldiers Aren't Playthings," *Smithsonian*, August 1980

"Collectors Are Recapturing Their Youth With Toy Soldiers," *The New York Times*, November 20, 1983

Davenport, Elaine, "The Martial Art of Sergeant Forbes," *Now!*, December 24, 1979

Dornberg, John, "The Little Tin Soldiers of Kulmbach," *Museum*, September/October 1982

Forbes, Robert L. Interview by author. New York, N.Y., December 17, 2003

Fornwalt, Russell J., "Toy Soldiers March to Auction Victories," *Tri-State Trader*, August 14, 1982

Francis, David, "Old Toy Soldiers Gaining Ground," *Tri-State Trader*, December 4, 1982

Garratt, John G. *The World Encyclopedia of Model Soldiers*. New York: The Overlook Press, 1981

Goldman, Michael, "Tin Toys and Toy Soldiers," *Diversion*, May 1982

Gropman, Donald, "Malcolm Forbes: Toy Soldiers' Commander-in-Chief," *Collectibles Illustrated*, May/June1983

Johnson, Peter, "A Heyde Tiger Hunt for Christmas," *Antique Finder*, November 1979

Johnson, Peter, "A Letter to Malcolm S. Forbes," May 8, 1984

Johnson, Peter, "Malcolm Forbes' Private Army," *Marbella Life*, Winter 1995–96

Johnson, Peter, "The Forbes Collection," *Military Modelling*, November 1979

Johnson, Peter. *Toy Armies*. London: B.T. Batsford Ltd., 1981

Kurtz, Henry I., "Toy Soldiers Never Die, They Just Turn to Profit," *American Way*, December 1979

"Military Moves," *Art & Antiques Weekly*, December 12–18, 1980

Olsen, Catherine, "And Their Bullets Were Made of Lead . . . ," *The Standard*, November 4, 1981

Porter, Bruce, "Toy Soldiers Never Die," *Connoisseur*, January 1986

Reif, Rita, "The New Rage for Old Toys," *House & Garden*, November 1981

Reif, Rita, *The New York Times*, July 25, 1982

Sells, Terry, "Manoil Toys: A History," *Old Toy Soldier Newsletter*, December 1979